WE ARE ALL
MITAKUYE OWASIN

WE ARE ALL RELATED
Mitakuye Owasin

1st printing. Printed in 2020

For more information, please contact:
Jessie Rencountre
www.jessie.rencountre.com
jrencountre@gmail.com

ISBN: 9798550272688

Printed in the United States

There is an ancient teaching by the Lakota, better known as the Sioux Indians of the Plains Regions of North America. This teaching says that we are related to everything. We use the phrase at the end of a prayer or as a prayer on its own. We say "MITAKUYE OWASIN" (pronounced "Me-da-ku-ye Oh-wa-say"). This teaching is used in many Lakota stories to remind us that everything is connected.

TO MY 4 DAUGHTERS AND ALL OF THE
THE CHILDREN WHO READ THIS BOOK,
MAY YOU ALWAYS REMEMBER THE
THE KNOWLEDGE THAT WE ARE ALL
BORN WITH KNOWING...

"MITAKUYE OWASIN"

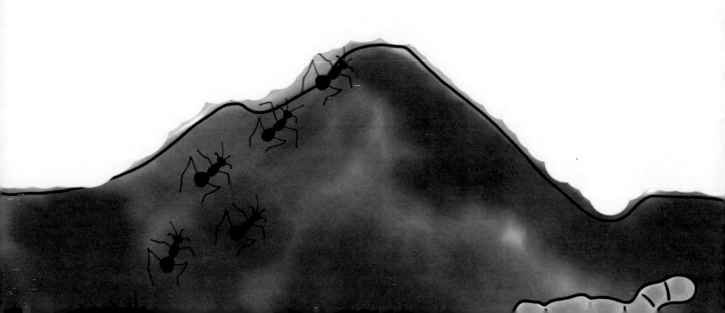

Every living thing was created by one Creator.

Because we were all created by one Creator, when we see all the different life in the water, we say...

"ALL MY RELATIVES"

When we see the winged nation, the ones who soar in the sky, we say...

"ALL MY RELATIVES"

When we see the plant nation, the ones that provide us with food and medicine for our bodies, we say...

"ALL MY RELATIVES"

When we see the animal nation, the ones with fur, horns, and paws, we say....

"ALL MY RELATIVES"

When we see the small crawlers, the ones that are busy and tiny, we say...

"ALL MY RELATIVES"

When we see our sisters and brothers of all different skin colors and cultures, we say...

"ALL MY RELATIVES"

When we see the moon, sun, stars, planets, and galaxies, we say...

"ALL MY RELATIVES"

We are connected and equal to every living thing in the Universe, this is why we are kind to...

"ALL MY RELATIVES"

About the Author

Jessie is a Hunkpapa Lakota from the Standing Rock Sioux Tribe. She grew up around her culture and has been influenced by Lakota values passed down to her from her parents and grandparents. She has spent the majority of her career working as a school counselor with elementary and high school students. She is the mother to Jaylee, Sophia Sadie, and Mila. Her experience of working with children, being a mother, and growing up around her Lakota culture have been big inspirations for her to write books for children. Jessie and her husband Whitney make their home with their daughters in the Black Hills of South Dakota.

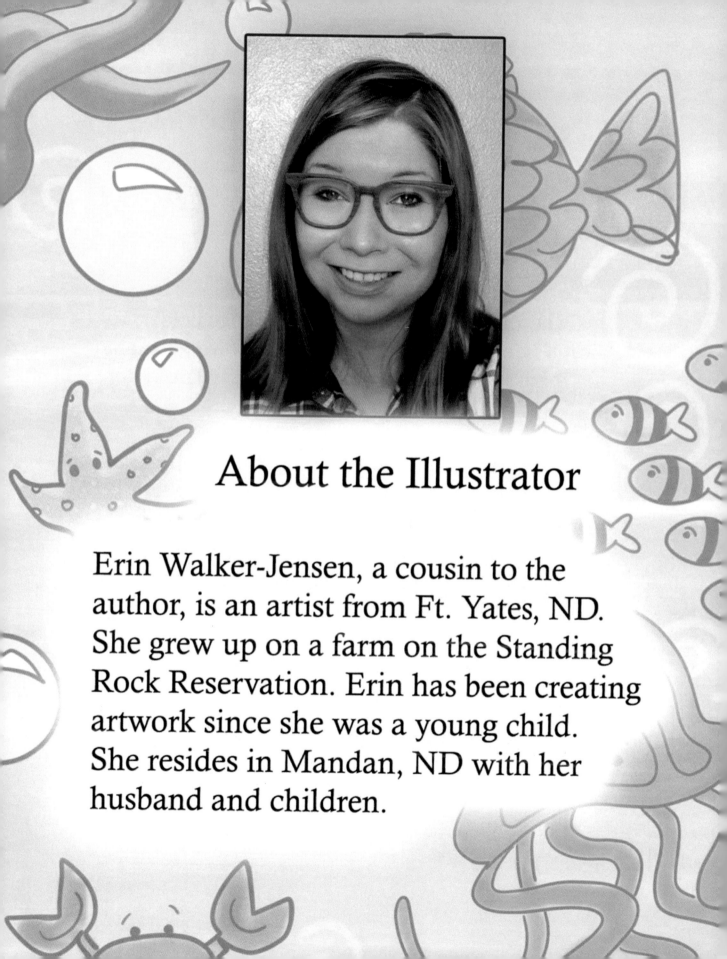

About the Illustrator

Erin Walker-Jensen, a cousin to the author, is an artist from Ft. Yates, ND. She grew up on a farm on the Standing Rock Reservation. Erin has been creating artwork since she was a young child. She resides in Mandan, ND with her husband and children.

THANK YOU

To all of our Lakota Cultural knowledge holders for instilling ancient knowledge on to the next generation. This is how our culture has been passed down for thousands of years.

To my parents for not only raising me with our Lakota values, but most importantly living with these values as an example.

To my wonderful husband for always encouraging me and helping me see my potential.

To my beautiful daughters for being some of the greatest teachers I have in life.

Made in the USA
Las Vegas, NV
19 November 2023

81040058R00017